our beautiful year

our beautiful year

_____ & _____

year _____

WELCOME

I want to begin by thanking you for picking up this book and welcoming you into something a little different from your average memory book. If you're a parent already and are anything like me, then you will have certain memories, phrases and words that you kept meaning to write down and maybe just never got around to. That's where I hope this book will not only spark creativity with your little one, but also prompt you to write down the things that you possibly never got around to! If you're about to become a parent for the first time, then I hope this will become a wonderful place for all your new memories.

The first half of the book is filled with activities and prompts that you can fill in with your child (if they're old enough) any time of the year. I've written these so that if you'd like to complete these each year, you can easily see how your little one is growing up and their amazing personality is developing.

The second half is organised by month and will take you through the year for seasonal moments to celebrate. Of course, if you've bought this not at the start of the year, you can begin at the month you're in and work your way through to January. This book is yours to use as suits you best!

I created this book as a unique gift that you can keep forever. I hope you enjoy it and build a beautiful collection so you can see how your child grows and changes over the years.

Now, let's get started!

Love,

Liana & Koazy xxx

WHO AM I?

First, there is one important thing to do.
Let's make a note here of who you are!

My eyes are:

....

My hair is:

....

I enjoy:

....

Here you can encourage your child to draw a picture of themselves – don't worry if they can't yet, it will be fun to see the changes they make each year. If you'd prefer to use a photo, you can stick that on this page, instead.

OUR FAMILY

Some families are big, others are small. Use the leaves on the tree below to write the names of the people you love:

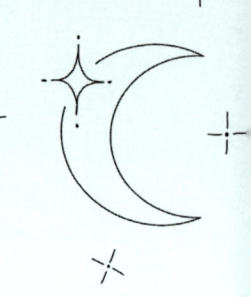

CHANGES

A lot can change in one short year . . .
let's make a note of what you love at the moment.

Encourage your little one to answer the questions below and write their response word for word (no matter how silly).

What is
your name?

How old
are you?

Who's your
best friend?

What makes
you happy?

What's your
favourite food?

What's your
favourite colour?

AWAY FROM HOME

Going on a trip can be very exciting! Sometimes we travel far away and sometimes we stay closer to home. Where did we go this time?

Colour in or circle how we got there:

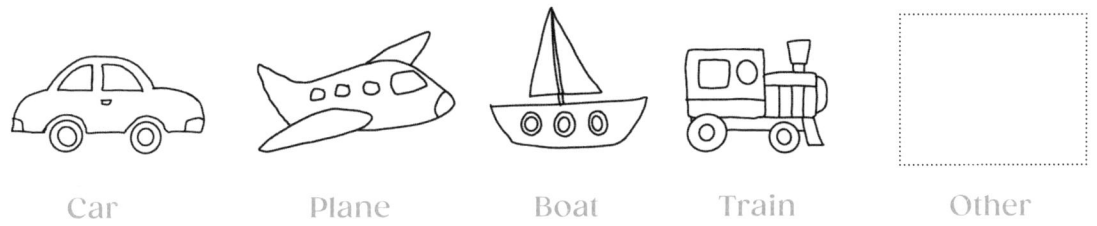

| Car | Plane | Boat | Train | Other |

Make a note here of a bit of the holiday you really enjoyed:

Add a photo or souvenir (like a ticket) to remember your holiday here:

YOUR CUTEST
QUOTES & WEIRD WORDS

You always come out with the cutest little words and phrases!
Let's make a note here of your favourite things to say.

It's easy to forget to make notes of how your little one mispronounces words and comes out with the most ridiculous sayings! Use the spaces here to write these down so you don't forget!

FAVOURITES PAGE

Let's write down all your favourite things at the moment.

Colour:

Food:

Toy:

Book:

Drink:

Game:

Show:

Animal:

Place:

Song:

Word/phrase:

MY FAVOURITE OUTFIT

You may already have a favourite outfit or costume that you love to wear! If you do, use the space below to draw it or add a photo.

Why is this your favourite outfit?

OUR ROUTINE

It's funny how we often don't notice changes in our routine.
How have our days looked recently? Write some notes here,
as it will be interesting to compare them to next year.

Morning:

Afternoon:

Evening:

BIRTHDAY PAGE

Happy birthday! Today is your special day. Let's make some notes here to remember how you spent it:

Today I turn .... years old.

How did you celebrate?

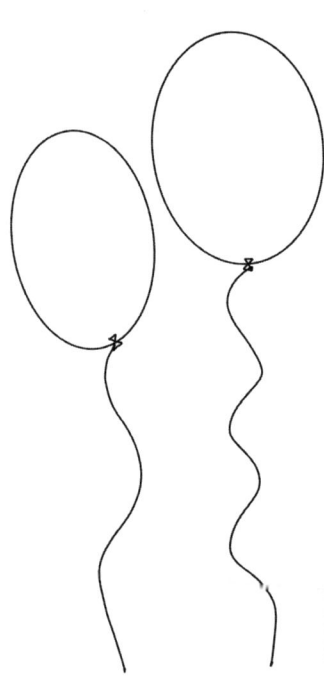
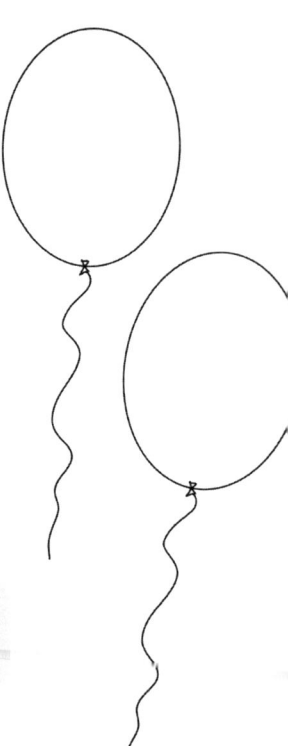

What did you want for your birthday?

My favourite present was:

Who came to visit?

What was your favourite thing to eat?

LETTER TO YOUR CHILD

Below is lots of space for you to write a letter to your little one – maybe something you want them to read next year, or maybe something you want them to read beyond that! Either way, use the space how you please.

JANUARY

TIME GOES SO FAST AND YOU'RE CHANGING ALL THE TIME

Here are some things you have said or done this month that have made me happy:

We've listened and sung along to lots of songs but our favourite song this month is:

We've had so many tasty meals but our favourite meal to eat this month is:

by

We celebrated _____'s birthday and our favourite moment on the day was:

A few of your favourite things from this month:

Trips! This month, we went to:

and we really enjoyed:

A funny question you asked me this month was:

A LOOK INSIDE YOUR CLOSET

The weather this month has been so cold, this is the outfit you're wearing today:

If your little one isn't able to draw yet, you can sketch in this space, too. Or add a photo, if you'd prefer.

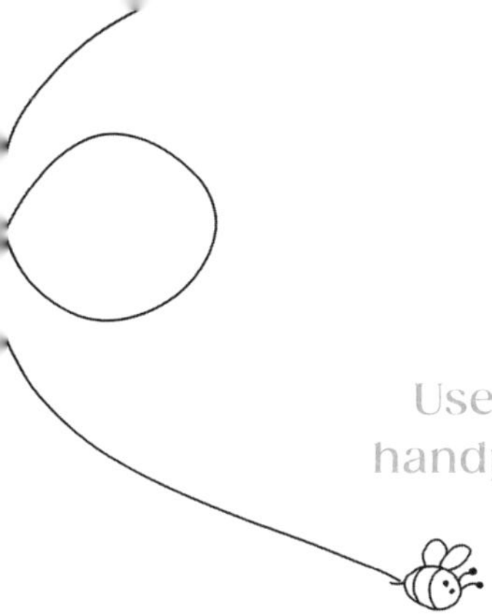

MAKE YOUR MARK

Use the space below to make a heart using your handprints – what colour are you going to choose?

It's easiest to do one hand at a time, and have their thumbs lined up with the middle of the heart shape.

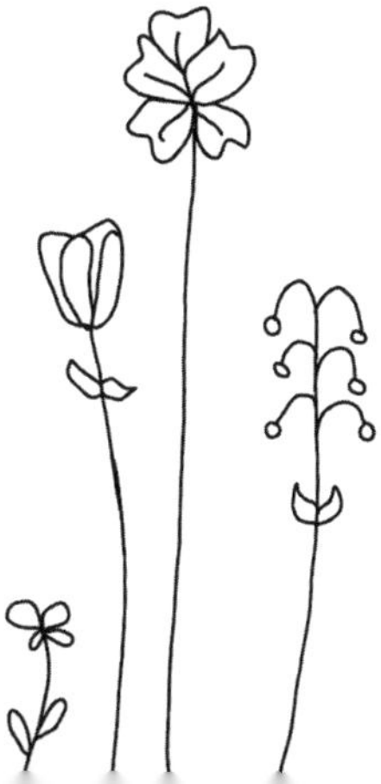

WHAT'S THE WEATHER?

What's the weather like this month? Draw the weather for today through the window below.

MOVIE NIGHT

There is nothing like a film and a snuggle on a cold evening!
Pick a movie for us to watch together and let's give it a rating.

We watched:

Rating:

*This is one for parents. How long
did your little one watch it for:*

*You could even
cook or bake a dish
together inspired
by the movie
you choose!*

FEBRUARY

TIME GOES SO FAST AND YOU'RE CHANGING ALL THE TIME

Here are some things you have said or done this month that have made me happy:

We've listened and sung along to lots of songs but our favourite song this month is:

We've had so many tasty meals but our favourite meal to eat this month is:

by

We celebrated _____'s birthday and our favourite moment on the day was:

A few of your favourite things from this month:

Trips! This month, we went to:

and we really enjoyed:

A funny question you asked me this month was:

VALENTINE'S DAY DATE

It can be fun to eat something special or something heart-shaped or pink to celebrate Valentine's Day. What did you eat this Valentine's Day? Write or draw what you had on this plate.

HEART TO HEART

This month is full of LOVE! Fill in the hearts below to say who you love and why.

Either you and/or your little one can fill in these hearts however you like; with colour, names and reasons why they're loved!

PANCAKE DAY

Pancake Day is a great opportunity to get your little one involved in the kitchen! Here is a recipe that you'll absolutely love.

Sometimes Pancake Day is in February, but it might also be in March, depending on the year. Come back to this page if it happens to fall later when you're filling out the book.

1 banana
1 egg
Dash of milk
2–4 tbsp Plain flour
Oil, for frying

1. Get a mixing bowl, add the banana and mash with a fork.

2. Add the egg and milk, and mix well.

3. Then gradually add the flour spoonful by spoonful until you reach your desired consistency – this will depend on whether you like your pancakes thinner or thicker.

4. Heat a frying pan on the hob and add a little oil if needed. Then add a dollop of the pancake mixture and cook until it is golden on the bottom side. Then, flip the pancake and wait until the other side is golden too. Repeat 3 to 4 times (depending on the size of your pancakes).

5. Serve immediately.

PANCAKE TOPPINGS

Can you use the drawing below to draw some of your favourite toppings?

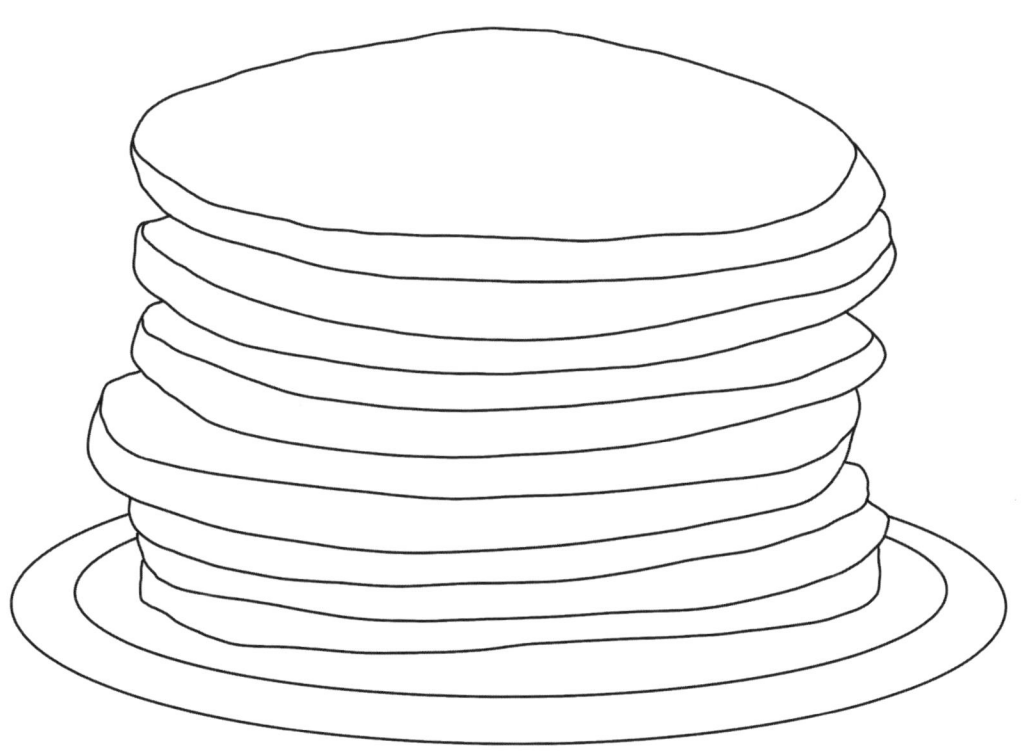

MARCH

TIME GOES SO FAST AND YOU'RE CHANGING ALL THE TIME

Here are some things you have said or done this month that have made me happy:

We've listened and sung along to lots of songs but our favourite song this month is:

by

We've had so many tasty meals but our favourite meal to eat this month is:

We celebrated _____'s birthday and our favourite moment on the day was:

A few of your favourite things from this month:

Trips! This month, we went to:

and we really enjoyed:

A funny question you asked me this month was:

WORLD BOOK DAY

It's World Book Day this month and that's the perfect excuse to dress up as your favourite character. If you don't like wearing costumes, you can draw your favourite character instead.

You really like it when we read:

The author of this book is:

If you dressed up, who did you go as?

Why is this character your favourite?

MOTHER'S DAY

This month we celebrate Mother's Day! Below is some space for you to write about an inspirational woman in your life.

Their name or nickname:

Why does she inspire you?

LOOK UP

It can be easy to forget to look up sometimes. Being careful not to look at the sun, make a note of what you see when you look up, both in daytime and nighttime.

WHAT MAKES YOU LAUGH?

It's so important to have a giggle every day!
What makes you laugh at the moment?

This could be a silly little game you play together, or it could be a TV show or character. It's such a lovely thing to compare each year.

APRIL

TIME GOES SO FAST AND YOU'RE CHANGING ALL THE TIME

Here are some things you have said or done this month that have made me happy:

We've listened and sung along to lots of songs but our favourite song this month is:

by

We've had so many tasty meals but our favourite meal to eat this month is:

We celebrated _____'s birthday and our favourite moment on the day was:

A few of your favourite things from this month:

Trips! This month, we went to:

and we really enjoyed:

A funny question you asked me this month was:

EASTER

Happy Easter! Below is a space to colour and decorate your own Easter eggs.

Easter can be in March or April, depending on the year. Come back to this page if it falls earlier when you're filling out the book.

EASTER EGG HUNT

An Easter Egg hunt can be so much fun.
Let's make a note of our own one here.

*Use this template below to record where you hid the
Easter eggs for your little one.*

I bet this hunt is making you think, if you would like your next clue head to the kitchen _____

Next, head to the _____, an egg might be waiting for you.

Make your way to the _____ next. You'll have to look hard though!

Our final stop! Go to the _____ and see if you can find anything exciting hidden there.

That was so much fun! How many eggs did you collect?

_____

LET'S GET MOVING

It's really fun to move our bodies however we can.
What do you like to do to get moving?

KNOCK KNOCK...

Have you ever written a joke? If so, make a note of it here.
If not, write down your favourite joke instead. The sillier the better!

MAy

TIME GOES SO FAST AND YOU'RE CHANGING ALL THE TIME

Here are some things you have said or done this month that have made me happy:

We've listened and sung along to lots of songs but our favourite song this month is:

by

We've had so many tasty meals but our favourite meal to eat this month is:

EXPLORING OUTDOORS

I'm sure you are spending a lot more time outside now, and the flowers are starting to spring up! Can you find your favourite flower and stick it in below?

It's best to press the flower before you stick it down. Open a heavy book in the middle and cover the pages with newspaper. Place your flower on the paper and then carefully close the book. You can weigh it down with more heavy books if needed. Then store the books in a warm, dry place and check your flower daily. Once dry, remove and stick here.

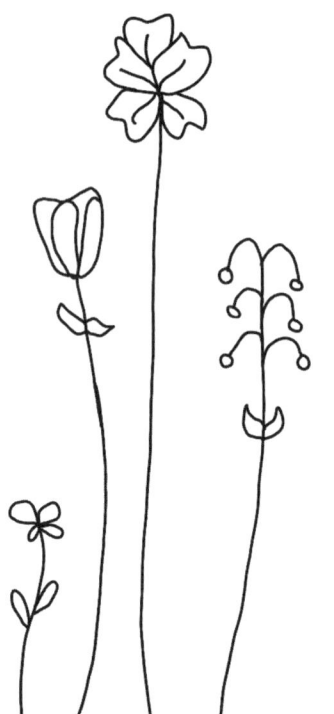

MAKE A NATURE BRACELET

Let's go outside and collect some flowers and leaves to create our very own nature bracelet.

A fun idea for a day outdoors – you can wrap a piece of Sellotape around your little one's wrist inside out to make a 'nature bracelet' by collecting leaves and flowers and sticking them on! You can then stick it down here to keep forever.

OUT AND ABOUT

Let's go on a walk! Let's try to answer these questions while we're outside.

Our favourite walk to go on is:

Did we see any animals?

yes   no

What was your favourite leaf that you saw?

How was the weather?

What was your favourite part?

How long did our walk take?

Don't worry if your child can't answer all the questions. Another fun thing to do is go on a colour walk. Choose a colour and try to spot as many things in that shade as you can!

WHAT'S THE WEATHER?

With the seasons changing, what's the weather like this month?
Draw what you can see through the window.

JUNE

TIME GOES SO FAST AND YOU'RE CHANGING ALL THE TIME

Here are some things you have said or done this month that have made me happy:

We've listened and sung along to lots of songs but our favourite song this month is:

by

We've had so many tasty meals but our favourite meal to eat this month is:

We celebrated _____'s birthday and our favourite moment on the day was:

A few of your favourite things from this month:

Trips! This month, we went to:

and we really enjoyed:

A funny question you asked me this month was:

FATHER'S DAY

This month we celebrate Father's Day! What do you love most about the father figure in your life?

Their name or nickname:

Why does he inspire you?

WORLD ENVIRONMENT DAY

It's so important to look after our environment, and this month it is World Environment Day! If you need some inspiration, here are a few fun ways you can celebrate this day.

- *Use recycled bits from your home to make something fun and creative! For example, you can make bottle-top fish by painting the bottle top, adding a googly eye, sticking it onto a piece of card and drawing a tail behind it.*

- *You could also fill a tuff tray or similar container with water and toys, and encourage your little one to 'clean the water' using a small net.*

We help protect the environment by _____

We love the environment because _____

We celebrated today by _____

CELEBRATE INSECT WEEK

It's Insect Week in June and it's so important to protect our bugs, which do so much to keep the natural world moving.

Do you like bugs?   yes ☐   no ☐

Draw your favourite type of bug here:

BUG SCAVENGER HUNT

Go outside and see what bugs you can spot.
Make a note of them here inside the magnifying glass.

JULY

TIME GOES SO FAST AND YOU'RE CHANGING ALL THE TIME

Here are some things you have said or done this month that have made me happy:

We've listened and sung along to lots of songs but our favourite song this month is:

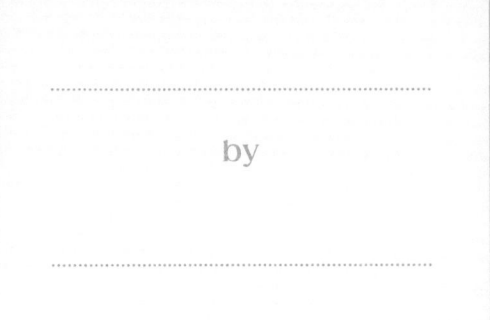

by

We've had so many tasty meals but our favourite meal to eat this month is:

We celebrated _____'s birthday and our favourite moment on the day was:

A few of your favourite things from this month:

Trips! This month, we went to:

and we really enjoyed:

A funny question you asked me this month was:

INTERNATIONAL FRIENDSHIP MONTH

July is all about friendship, as it's International Friendship Month! Who are your best friends?

PERFECT PICNIC

The weather is normally getting better at this time of year, which means it's the perfect time for a picnic! Add to the blanket below your favourite things to eat outside.

YOUR STUFFIE'S BIRTHDAY

We've all heard of a teddy bear's picnic, but have you heard of a stuffie's birthday? It's important to celebrate the birthdays of your stuffed animals as well as your own!

What's the name of your stuffie?

How old are they?

They were bought for you by:

We celebrated their birthday by:

This doesn't need to be anything over the top – you could celebrate with a fairy cake with a candle or make teddy-sized birthday hats with some paper and glue. With lots of singing, it's such a fun activity!

MAKE YOUR MARK

Use the space below to create a butterfly with your handprints. You could use lots of your favourite colours to create a really beautiful butterfly.

AUGUST

TIME GOES SO FAST AND YOU'RE CHANGING ALL THE TIME

Here are some things you have said or done this month that have made me happy:

We've listened and sung along to lots of songs but our favourite song this month is:

by

We've had so many tasty meals but our favourite meal to eat this month is:

BLACKBERRY BUSHES

With any luck the blackberry bushes should be full of fruit now. Do you have any nearby? Have you been able to go and pick any? In the space below, use a squished berry as ink to make fingerprint berries. If you didn't pick blackberries, did you pick any other fruit?

If you don't have any blackberries growing near you, you could buy some from the supermarket and use one here (and eat the rest).

OUR FAMILY TRIP

Did we go on any trips this month? Use the space below to write all about it or add a photo or souvenir from the trip.

We went to _____ _____

We were on holiday from __ / __ / __ to __ / __ / __

BBQ SEASON

BBQ season is in full swing! What is your idea of a perfect BBQ?
Write down all your favourite things you love to eat here.

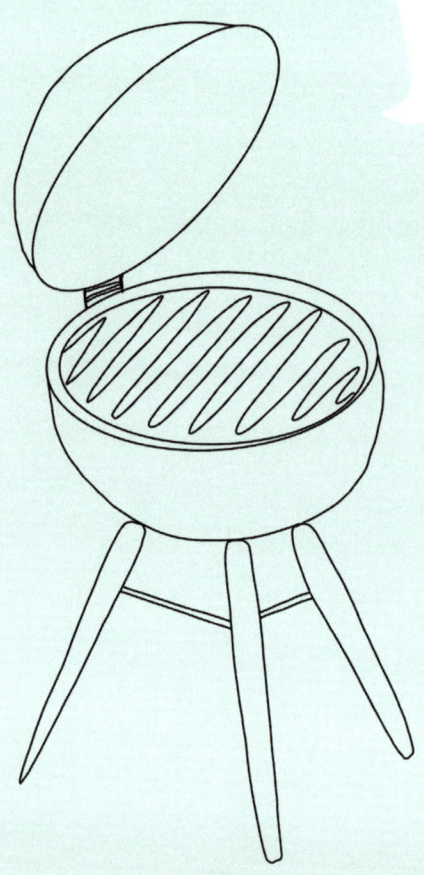

HEAD CHEF

Who's in charge when you have a BBQ? Make some notes here about why they're the head chef of the BBQ this year.

Our BBQ chef is

....

They're really good at making

....

They get to be in charge because

....

SEPTEMBER

TIME GOES SO FAST AND YOU'RE CHANGING ALL THE TIME

Here are some things you have said or done this month that have made me happy:

We've listened and sung along to lots of songs but our favourite song this month is:

by

We've had so many tasty meals but our favourite meal to eat this month is:

We celebrated _____'s birthday and our favourite moment on the day was:

A few of your favourite things from this month:

Trips! This month, we went to:

and we really enjoyed:

A funny question you asked me this month was:

BACK TO SCHOOL

It's time to go back to school or nursery. Make a note here of some of your favourite things about this month.

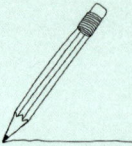

What do you love most about school or nursery?

Has anything changed since last year?

It could be really fun to find out what your little one thinks you do while they're at school, ask your child:

What does Mummy do for work?

What does Daddy do for work?

THINGS TO LOVE ABOUT SCHOOL

There's so much to love about going to school or nursery.
Use this page to write down the things you love the most.

My favourite subject is: My favourite teacher is:

During class, I sit next to:

ALL DRESSED UP

If you're old enough, you might be wearing a uniform now! Either way, let's add a photo here of you ready for school or nursery. You're growing up so fast!

WITH MY FRIENDS

One of the best things about going back to school or nursery is getting to see your friends again. Let's add a photo of you all together.

It's a good idea to write the names of each of the children in the photo, so you can remember in years to come!

OCTOBER

TIME GOES SO FAST AND YOU'RE CHANGING ALL THE TIME

Here are some things you have said or done this month that have made me happy:

We've listened and sung along to lots of songs but our favourite song this month is:

We've had so many tasty meals but our favourite meal to eat this month is:

by

We celebrated _____'s birthday and our favourite moment on the day was:

A few of your favourite things from this month:

Trips! This month, we went to:

and we really enjoyed:

A funny question you asked me this month was:

HALLOWEEN

It's spooky time this month! This is the outfit that you wore:

Use this space to draw or add a photo of your little one in their scariest costume.

OUR PUMPKIN DESIGN

Here is a pumpkin for you to add your own spooky design to. Remember, the scarier the better!

A perfect way to spend spooky season is to go pumpkin picking! You could encourage your little one to choose whichever pumpkin they like (no matter how ridiculous), then carve or paint it together.

MAKE YOUR MARK

Create your own personal pumpkin here.

Paint your little one's hand orange and then turn the book upside down so the green stalk and leaves line up with the bottom of your child's hand. You'll be left with a lovely pumpkin shape!

APPLE DAY

Did you know about Apple Day? Well, you do now!
Here's how to make your very own apple bird feeder.

1 apple
string
2 sticks
sunflower
or pumpkin
seeds

1. Remove the core of the apple (if you don't have an apple corer, you could use a hard stick or screwdriver to make a hole down the middle – be careful!).

2. Tie the string around the middle of your first stick, then thread the string through the hole, from the bottom to the top of the apple. You'll use the excess string to tie your feeder onto a tree branch.

3. Next, push your second stick all the way through the bottom of the apple, at a right angle to the stick on the string. This creates an x-shaped perch for the birds.

4. Stick your sunflower seeds into the apple, all over.

5. Hang your feeder on a strong branch, high enough off the ground for the birds to feed safely, away from predators!

We hope you get lots of feathered visitors!

NOVEMBER

TIME GOES SO FAST AND YOU'RE CHANGING ALL THE TIME

Here are some things you have said or done this month that have made me happy:

We've listened and sung along to lots of songs but our favourite song this month is:

We've had so many tasty meals but our favourite meal to eat this month is:

by

We celebrated _____'s birthday and our favourite moment on the day was:

A few of your favourite things from this month:

Trips! This month, we went to:

and we really enjoyed:

A funny question you asked me this month was:

BONFIRE NIGHT

This month may be a little loud with all the fireworks, use the space below to draw your own.

WORLD KINDNESS DAY

It's World Kindness Day! Although it's important to be kind every day, what little things have you done this month to show kindness to others?

You can use this opportunity to tell your little one about all the small gestures they have made that are incredibly kind, for example, sharing a toy.

OUR GRATITUDE LIST

It's really lovely to remember to be grateful for the little and big things that we have. Let's make a list here of everything we're grateful for:

You could also write the things you're grateful for as a family.

SING-A-LONG

Do you like to listen to music? Make a note in the space below of who your favourite band or singer is at the moment. You can also write your favourite song and lyric!

DECEMBER

TIME GOES SO FAST AND YOU'RE CHANGING ALL THE TIME

Here are some things you have said or done this month that have made me happy:

We've listened and sung along to lots of songs but our favourite song this month is:

We've had so many tasty meals but our favourite meal to eat this month is:

by

We celebrated _____'s birthday and our favourite moment on the day was:

A few of your favourite things from this month:

Trips! This month, we went to:

and we really enjoyed:

A funny question you asked me this month was:

CHRISTMAS

We are so close to Christmas!

Use the page below to write your own letter to Father Christmas.

Dear Father Christmas,

CHRISTMAS TREE

The tree below is very bare, could you help decorate it?

OUR CHRISTMAS

Use this page to make a note of how we spent our Christmas Day.

We ate our Christmas meal at
....

We had
....
....

We celebrated Christmas this year with
....
....

We watched
....
....

I was really lucky and received these lovely gifts:
....
....
....

SNOW DAYS

Did it snow this year? My snowman is called:

Create your own snowman below!

D

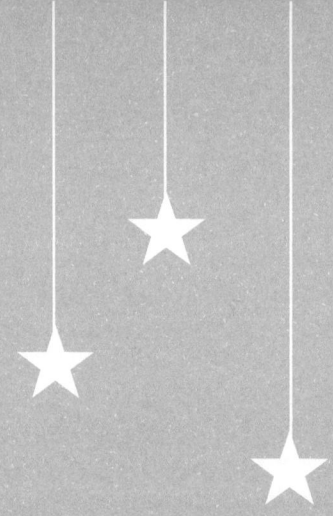

OUR PHOTO ALBUM

Use this section of the book to add any extra photos you want to keep safe and look at in years to come. You could also add any extra souvenirs from trips or drawings your little one has done . . . make these pages your own!

EBURY PRESS

UK | USA | Canada | Ireland | Australia
India | New Zealand | South Africa

Ebury Press is part of the Penguin Random House group of companies whose addresses can be found at global.penguinrandomhouse.com

Penguin Random House UK
One Embassy Gardens, 8 Viaduct Gardens, London SW11 7BW

penguin.co.uk
global.penguinrandomhouse.com

First published by Ebury Press in 2025

1

Copyright © Liana Jade and Connor Darlington 2025
Illustrations © Hart Studio 2025

The moral right of the author has been asserted.

Penguin Random House values and supports copyright. Copyright fuels creativity, encourages diverse voices, promotes freedom of expression and supports a vibrant culture. Thank you for purchasing an authorised edition of this book and for respecting intellectual property laws by not reproducing, scanning or distributing any part of it by any means without permission. You are supporting authors and enabling Penguin Random House to continue to publish books for everyone. No part of this book may be used or reproduced in any manner for the purpose of training artificial intelligence technologies or systems. In accordance with Article 4(3) of the DSM Directive 2019/790, Penguin Random House expressly reserves this work from the text and data mining exception.

Editorial Director: Ru Merritt
Senior Editor: Liv Nightingall
Production Director: Catherine Ngwong
Designer: Hart Studio

Colour origination by Altaimage Ltd
Printed and bound in Germany by Mohn Media

The authorised representative in the EEA is Penguin Random House Ireland, Morrison Chambers, 32 Nassau Street, Dublin D02 YH68.

A CIP catalogue record for this book is available from the British Library

ISBN 9781529968002

Penguin Random House is committed to a sustainable future for our business, our readers and our planet. This book is made from Forest Stewardship Council® certified paper.